Survival Guide

written by David Orme and Helen Bird

illustrated by Becky Blake and Jackie Harland

Contents

Introduction

Living in the wild is hard.

There might be lots of food one week, and only a little the next week. The weather keeps changing. And there is always the chance that something is lying in wait, ready to eat you!

Over millions of years, animals and plants have learned to live with whatever nature throws at them.

Now nature faces its biggest problem – the problem caused by man, the most successful **species** of all.

In the freezer

The frozen Arctic and Antarctic are hard places to live. And yet these parts of the world are full of life. In the Antarctic, penguins brave the ice and snow.

In the Arctic, the polar bear is a feared **predator**. On the land, plants have found their own way to survive. Each living thing has found its own special way to survive.

The Emperor penguins of the Antarctic huddle together in **colonies** *to keep warm.*

Case Study 1

Lichens

You may have seen grey or yellow marks that spread over roofs, tree trunks and old stone walls. These are lichens, one of the world's greatest survivors!

Lichens' special trick is to be two plants in one, an **alga** and a **fungus**.

How?

- *The alga and fungus work together to produce food so the lichen can live.*
- *Lichens can survive in very low temperatures.*

Lichens are very slow growing, and some are thought to be over 4,000 years old.

In the Arctic, a special lichen called reindeer moss is food for reindeer; without it reindeer would be unable to live in the Arctic.

Lichen

Reindeer moss

Polar bears

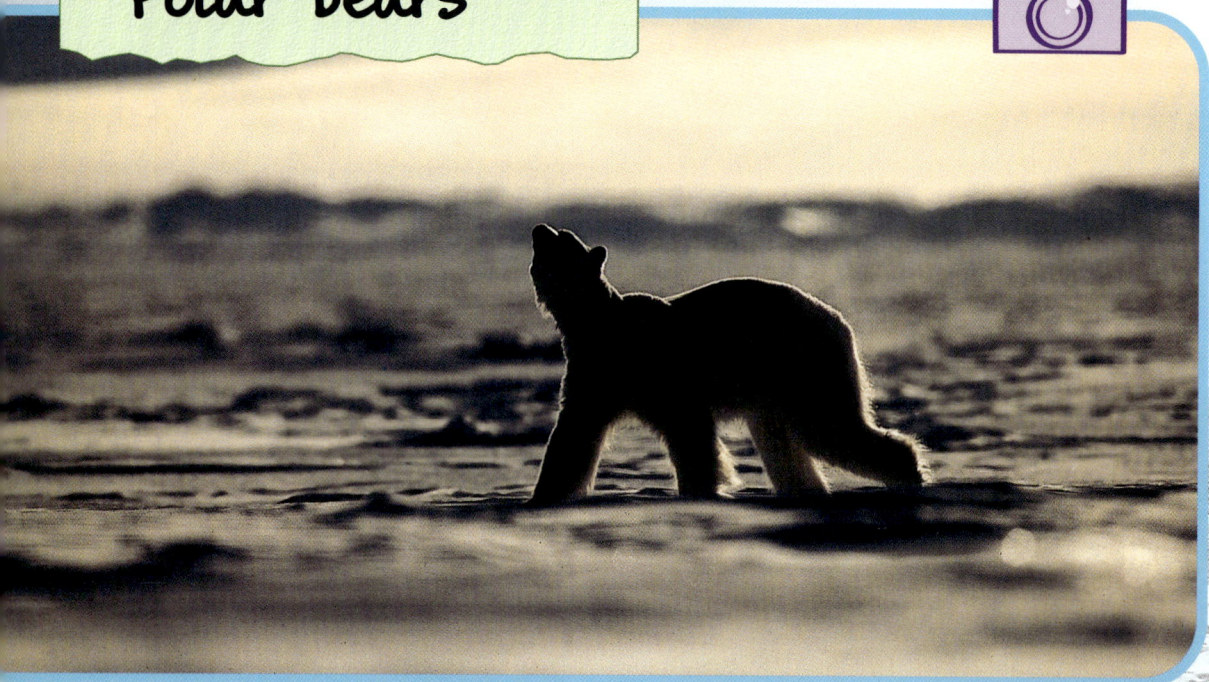

Polar bears are made for life in very cold places. Their thick fur keeps them **insulated** and warm. They have a strong sense of smell, which means they can smell **prey** from a long way away. Their powerful claws can kill a seal with one blow.

Arctic Region

Alaska

Canada

Russia

Arctic Ocean

North Pole

Greenland

Finland

Arctic Circle   Norway   Sweden

How
?

- A *strong sense of smell means they can smell prey from a long way away.*
- *Long, sharp claws to kill their prey.*
- *Thick, warm coat keeps them warm.*

Female polar bears give birth once every two years. When the cubs are born, they each weigh under one kilogram. It is a year before the cubs are strong enough to hunt for themselves.

7

Some like it hot

The world's deserts are another hard place to live. There is very little water. Temperatures are often higher than any animal could survive for long. Yet deserts do have plants and animals.

Lizards move quickly over hot surfaces so that their feet don't burn!

How do they survive?

Many animals spend the hottest parts of the day in **burrows**. They come out only in the cool of the evening or at night.

Plants grow thick skins and fleshy leaves that don't quickly wilt in the heat.

Kangaroo rats

- Nose absorbs moisture.
- Creates own water.
- Lives in cool undergroung den.

The kangaroo rat is made to survive desert life. During the day it lives in the cool of its underground den.

Kangaroo rats have very special noses which can absorb water from the air.

Kangaroo rats also have an amazing survival trick. They can create their own water from the driest of foods. In fact, they are so used to living in the desert, that they don't drink water even if they are given it!

Case Study 2
Barrel cacti

The cactus has to cope with great heat (and sometimes extreme cold, for deserts can be very cold at night). It has to survive with only a little water.

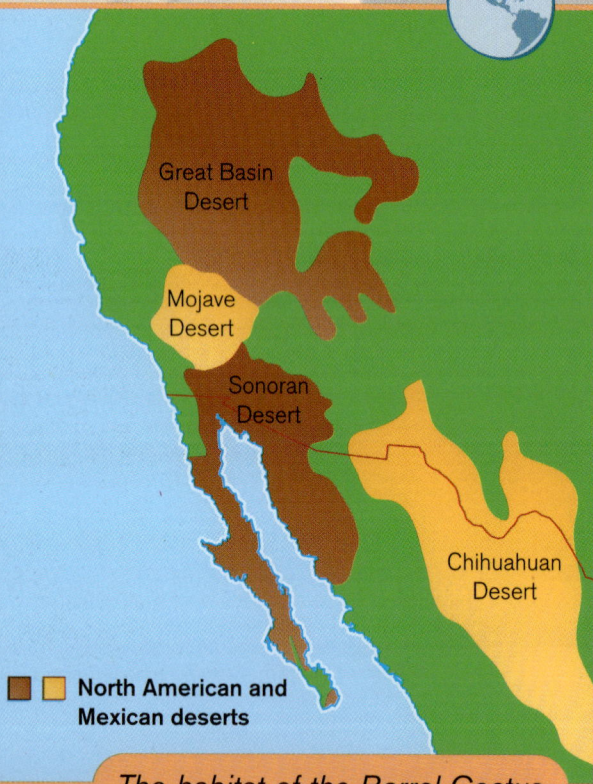

Great Basin Desert

Mojave Desert

Sonoran Desert

Chihuahuan Desert

North American and Mexican deserts

The habitat of the Barrel Cactus

In the hot desert, leaves would soon die, so the barrel cactus has none. It does have very long roots which capture as much water as possible.

The cactus uses its body to store water. Cacti can survive years of **drought** on the water collected from a single rainfall.

Everyone knows that cactus plants have spines!
The spines put off animals who want to eat the cactus.

How?

- Large roots spread out to collect water.
- Barrel-shaped body stores water.
- Spikes protect from animals.

In the dark

Darkness can be useful. If you can't be seen you can't be eaten! But there are problems, too.

In the dark, how do you move around without bumping into things?

How do you find a mate, or your next meal?

How can plants grow in the dark?

Yet even in the darkest places there is life. In total darkness where no light ever reaches, insects look for food such as the droppings from bats or birds. In the deepest parts of the oceans fish live in a world of total darkness.

Bats

During the day bats hide away in dark places such as caves, the trunks of rotten trees, or in the roofs of buildings. But when evening comes they are ready to start hunting for food.

How do they manage to fly in the dark without bumping into things?

Bats have small bodies, but huge ears. As they fly they make very high-pitched squeaks which are too high for most people to hear. The bats listen for the echoes of the squeaks to tell them where things are.

The main problem bats face now is finding places to live because modern buildings do not have as many dark hiding places as old ones did.

How ?

• *Huge ears provide very good hearing.*

At the bottom of the deepest oceans, it is black. Yet the fish that live there manage to survive.

In the total darkness at the bottom of the sea, you might think it would be hard to find a mate. The male anglerfish can sense a female fish from far away. Once he has found his mate, the male attaches his mouth to her body so he cannot lose her again!

One trick that deep sea fish have, is to make their own light! Light is made by chemical changes in the skin. Using this light, fish can even flash messages to each other!

The anglerfish has a "fishing rod" jutting out from its head. At the end of this rod there is a light. When a little fish arrives to see what is going on, the huge jaws of the anglerfish are waiting!

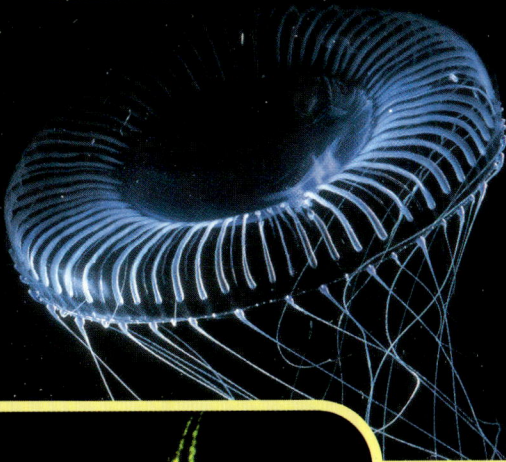

Some bioluminescent fish

- *Fishing rod style light attracts prey.*
- *Good sense of smell finds a mate.*

15

Not getting eaten

The most important survival problem for animals and plants is:

How do you avoid being eaten?

- You could be good at **camouflage**.
- You could run very fast to escape.
- You could have sharp teeth and claws to fight back.
- You could have spines to make yourself difficult to eat.
- You could make sure that you taste really bad so no one wants to eat you.

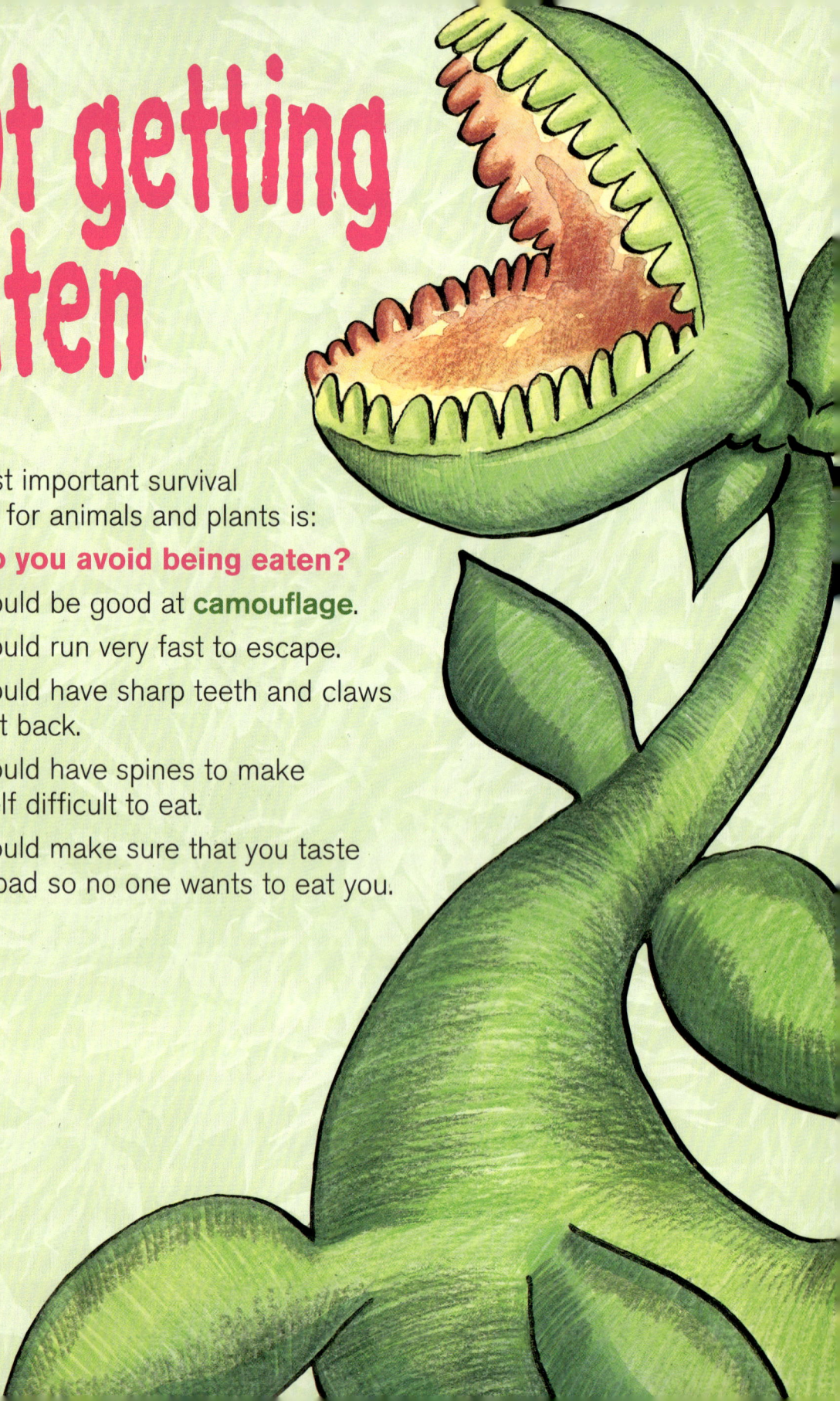

Sensitive plants

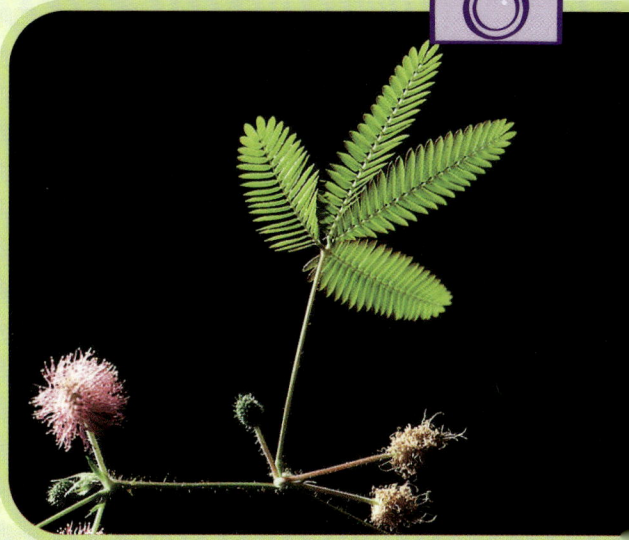

Many predators like to catch their prey live; they will ignore any dead creatures they may find. Some animals take advantage of this by "playing dead". A plant can do this, too! It is called a sensitive plant.

If you touch a sensitive plant the leaves will flop. What looked like a juicy leaf now looks dry and not worth eating!

This plant is very sensitive to vibration. The smallest touch of a finger will make them flop!

How?

- *Senses vibrations around it and flops to look dead.*

Case Study 2

Thompson's gazelle

It is a hot day in East Africa. A herd of Thompson's gazelle is feeding. On the edge of the herd young males are keeping watch for lions, hyenas and cheetahs.

One of the young males has sighted a predator! He shakes and stamps his feet in alarm.

No predator will attack the entire herd. It will try to pick off one single animal on the edge.

Now the predator is ready to attack. The gazelle will have to rely on its speed to avoid being eaten. It can run at 55 kilometres an hour (kph) for up to 15 minutes and can go as fast as 80 kph when running from predators. While it runs it takes great leaps in the air to see where it is going and to check where the predator is.

Sometimes the young males are caught and the predator has its meal, but the breeding females have been saved. One has died so many can live.

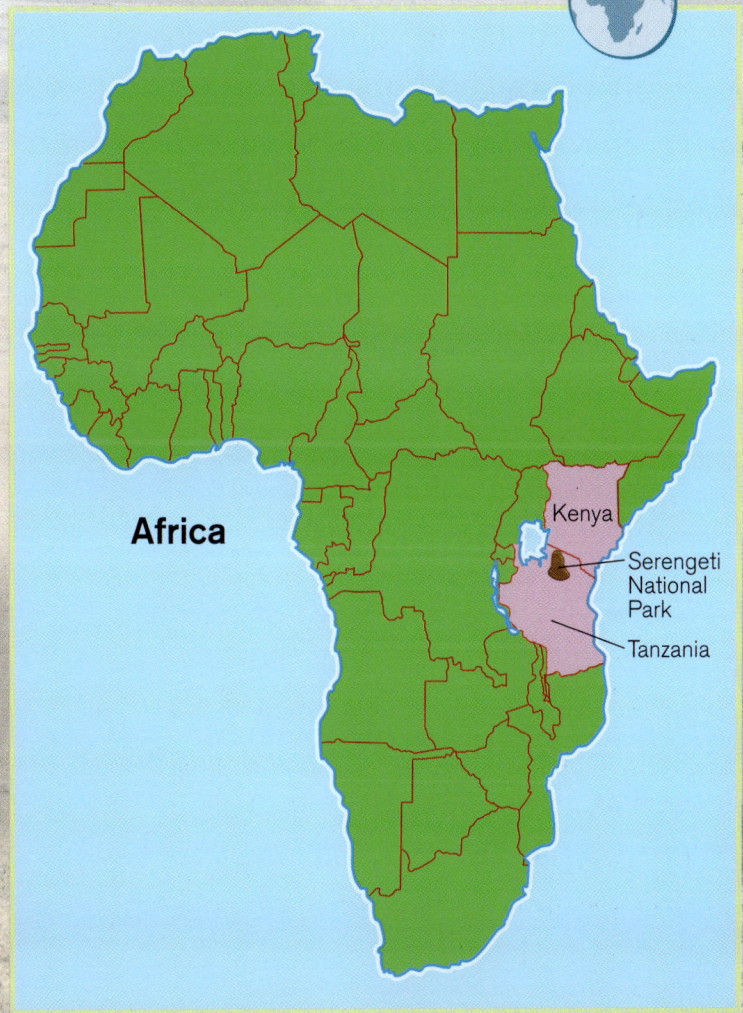

How ?

- *Sharp eyesight spots predators.*
- *Stick together in a herd for protection against predators.*
- *Run very fast to escape predators.*

Africa

Kenya

Serengeti National Park

Tanzania

Looking after baby

Survival is important for individual animals and plants, but survival of the whole species is even more important. To make sure the species survives all animals and plants have offspring.

But how can they be sure that the offspring will survive?

Many animals, like humans, look after their offspring for months or years, until the young are old enough to look after themselves. But for some living things, such as plants and many sea creatures, looking after their young is impossible. And so another trick is used: producing so many thousands of offspring that at least a few survive.

Most turtles produce up to 200 eggs at a time.

Rosebay willowherb

The rosebay willowherb is found everywhere.

One reason for the willowherb's great success is its method of spreading seeds. In the late summer thousands of its seeds, each with a feathery "sail", are blown by the wind. Most of them end up in places where they can't grow, but there are so many seeds that a few from each plant survive to grow and create new plants.

How ?

- *Produces thousands of seeds so some will have a chance of surviving.*

Case Study 2

Cuckoos

The cuckoo arrives in Britain from Africa in April, but it does not start nest building. Once other birds have built their nests and started to lay eggs, the cuckoo lays its own egg in their nest. The cuckoo can even make the colour and size of its egg match the eggs of the other bird.

Cuckoo chick being fed by foster parent

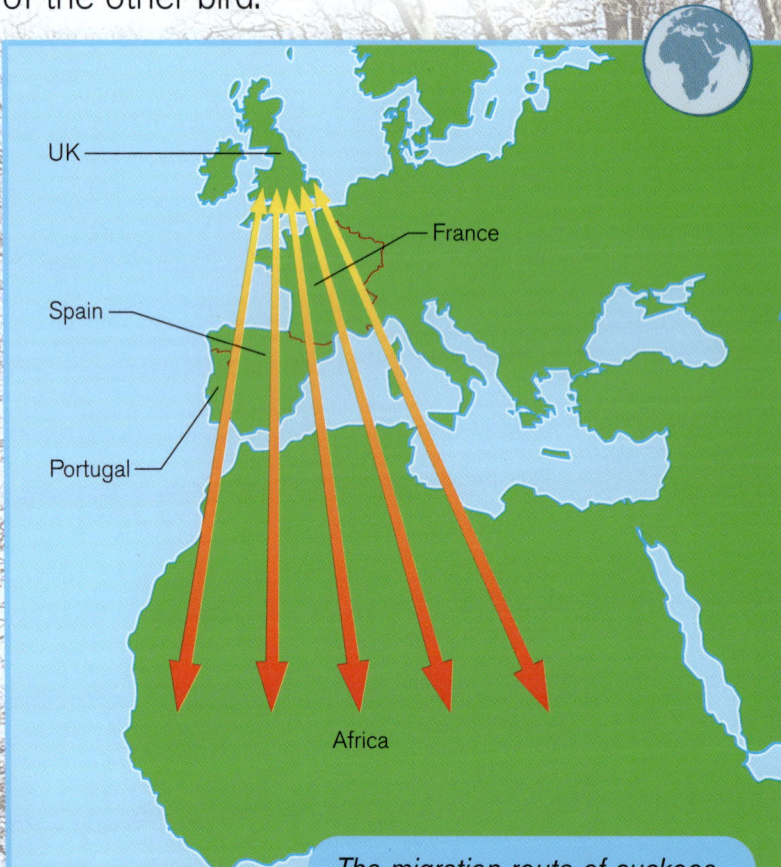

UK

France

Spain

Portugal

Africa

The migration route of cuckoos

Once they are hatched, the cuckoo chicks have another trick to make sure they survive. They have a sensitive patch on their backs, and if they feel something rubbing against it, they push hard to get rid of the tickle – so they push the other chicks out of the nest!

How
?

- "Foster" parents look after the chick until it is able to fly.

Surviving the seasons

The changing seasons are a big problem for animals and plants. In summer and autumn there is warmth and plenty of food, but when winter comes the warmth and food disappear.

Storing food for the winter and **hibernation** is the answer for some creatures; others, such as birds, travel to warmer places.

Annual plants survive as seeds buried safe in the ground; **perennial** plants need other ways to live through the winter. Some borrow a trick from animals – they hibernate underground!

Pets such as tortoises hibernate over the winter months.

Daffodils

How?

- New bulbs are made each year from the old bulbs.

Spring flowers like the daffodil grow leaves to make food, and flowers to make seeds, before the leaves of trees block out the sunlight.

There is plenty going on below ground as well. The daffodil leaves and flowers grow from an underground bulb or food store. As the old bulb gives up its food to build the plant, new bulbs are being made ready for next year's plants. The bulbs are not just a food store, but a way of creating new daffodil plants. Each bulb made will be a separate plant, ready to grow as soon as the winter is over.

Dormice

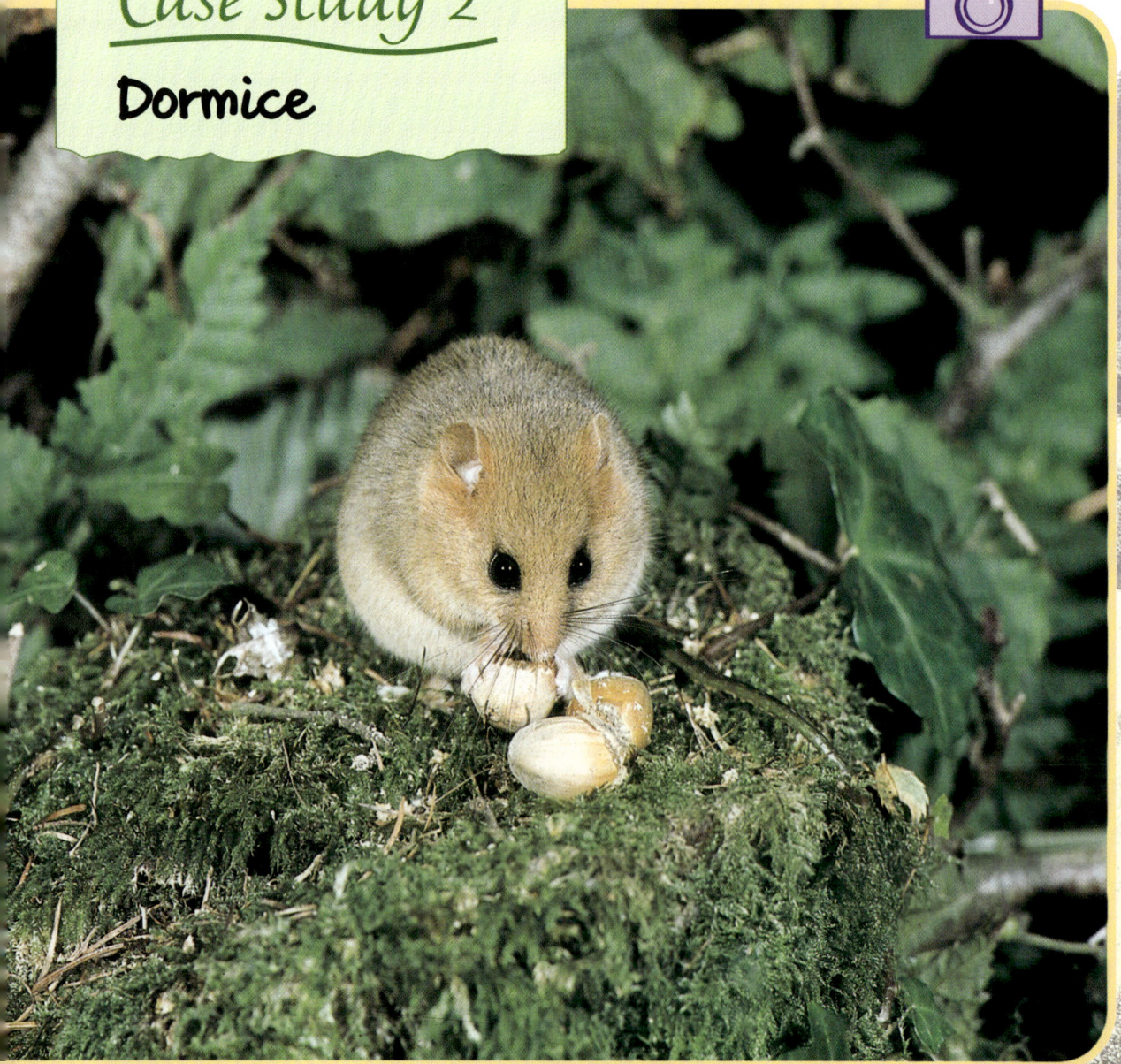

In the autumn the dormouse feeds all the time. The dormouse needs to build up the stores of fat in its body if it is to survive hibernation.

For a dormouse, hibernation can be very long – some animals have even been known to sleep for nine months at a time.

As soon as the colder weather arrives in October, the dormouse prepares its place to hibernate. It usually sleeps on the ground, rolled tightly into a ball in a nest of leaves and grass. Dormice usually sleep until the warmer weather of March or April. The life span of a dormouse is five years. This is a very long time for a creature of this size – they survive because they sleep so much!

How ?

- *Eats constantly in the autumn and stores up body fat.*
- *Sleeps for 6 months of the year or more!*

Changing habitats

Animals can adapt to some changes, such as drought and food shortage. But a major problem for animals is caused by people.

For example, some animals may lose their **habitat** when forests are cut down or wet places are drained.

Changes are hard for animals to cope with – but nature can still fight back!

Urban foxes

The fox was once a country animal. When changes to the countryside made life difficult for foxes, they found new places to live and breed – in the city!

Urban foxes are born in March in an **earth** which might be in a town park or garden. The first few weeks are dangerous times as the cubs are blind and helpless. But by October the young foxes will be big enough to find their own home.

In some ways the city is good for a growing fox because there is plenty of food all the year round.

This animal has found a new answer to the problem of survival in a changing world.

How ?

- *Moved to towns and cities where there is always plenty of food.*

Peppered moths

grey and speckled variety

black variety

In Victorian Britain many places were darkened by soot. This was bad news for light coloured insects – it was easier for birds to see them against the dark surface!

The peppered moth is unusual because it comes in two colours. One is grey and speckled and the other nearly black. In Victorian Britain, the black type became much more common, because this type blended into sooty surfaces and had a much better chance of survival.

Today smoke is much less of a problem and the population of peppered moths is changing again. The speckled peppered moth is on the increase.

How
?

• The type with the best colour for survival increases.

Glossary

alga a simple type of plant, for example seaweed

annual a plant that lasts for only one year

burrow a hole in the ground which an animal lives in

camouflage blending into the background

colony large group of one type of animal

drought period of little or no rainfall

earth a fox's home

fungus a type of plant that cannot make its own food, such as a mushroom

habitat place where an animal or plant lives

hibernation the ability of some animals to sleep through times when food is hard to find

insulate stop heat or cold passing through

maternity den a place prepared by an animal to give birth in

offspring young animals

perennial a plant that can live for a number of years

predator an animal that hunts and eats other animals

prey an animal hunted and eaten by another animal

species a particular kind of animal or plant

urban to do with towns and cities

Index